Two Little Witchlings series

SAMHAIN:
The Spirit Who
Came To Supper

Written & Illustrated by
Becky Susan Adams

Dedicated to Ruth Mathieson.
Fly high, Sister 🎩

It was October 31st and the Witchlings were carving pumpkins while Mama was decorating the dining room table with acorns, autumn leaves & pinecones. "I'm so excited to wear my costume!" declared Lily Witchling with a huge grin. "When we go trick-or-treating, I think I'm going to start on Maple Road. They always have the best soul cakes there!"
"Don't forget to say a prayer to the Goddess for those who hand out treats," Mama reminded her. "In exchange for a goodie, you say a blessing for the giver. Are you excited too, Rose?"
Rose Witchling gave a small smile.

When the pumpkins were done, Mama put a lit candle inside them & placed them next to the front door. "They will see off any bad spirits, & welcome any good ones for the Samhain Supper later," she smiled.

"Mama, why do we always have an empty seat at the table on Halloween?" Rose asked.

"This night is special, my love," came the reply. "It's when the veil between our world & the next is *really thin*, thin enough for spirits to come through. We leave an empty chair & plate for any ancestors who wish to come & dine with us this evening. Now, why don't you go get dressed for trick-or-treating?"

Rose went to her room & hid under her bed covers
with her torchlight. She didn't want to leave for
trick-or-treating. She didn't want to wear her
costume. She didn't want to go outside.
"Why are you hiding?" came a quiet voice.
Rose looked to the side & found a little ghost sitting
under the blanket next to her.
"Oh, it's nothing," she replied. "I just don't want to go
out this evening. It's too dark. I.. well, I.. I don't like
the dark."
"That's okay," smiled the little ghost. "I'm afraid of
the dark too. You never know what's in it, and it's
really big, & really, you know, *dark*."

"Wait a minute, how come you're in my house?" asked Rose Witchling.

"You invited me," the little ghost stated. "For the Samhain Supper. You left an empty chair for me. I'm just waiting for it to start."

"Well, you're in for a real treat," said Rose matter-of-factly. "My Mama is a *great* cook. But she & my Big Sister are going trick-or-treating first, so we have to wait a while."

"That's a shame, I'm really quite snacky," the spirit responded. "Maybe we could just go get one or two soul cakes from your neighbours? We can take this torch to keep us safe from the dark!"

Rose reluctantly agreed, & got her costume out of the wardrobe.

The sun had now gone to bed, but there were plenty of lanterns lit all along the village pathways. Rose was still a bit scared, so they hurried to the next house.

"Happy Hallows Eve!" said Tabitha, handing them both a soul cake. "What lovely costumes!"

"Thank you so much," said the little Witchling. "Do you need prayers?"

"Yes please," replied the troll. "My owl isn't feeling very well."

"Then may the Goddess bless your owl with good health," smiled Rose.

"*Thank you, child*," came a voice from above.

Rose looked up towards where the thank you had come from, & saw an owl sitting on the tree branch.

"You're very welcome!" she said. "But.. aren't you afraid of sitting in the dark like that?"

"On the contrary, small one," spoke the owl. "I do my best hunting in the dark. The yummiest snacks are the ones that don't see me coming."

"So you find the darkness helpful instead of scary?" asked the little ghost.

"Oh absolutely," replied the beautiful bird. "Very helpful indeed."

I guess the dark could be helpful, Rose thought to herself.

"That was delicious," grinned the little ghost, wiping the last crumbs from her face. "May we get another one?"

They walked on to Mr Brown's, who was adjusting a telescope he had set up.

"Ah, what *spirited* costumes!" said Mr Brown. "Come! There's a plate of soul cakes on the table, help yourselves. No need for a prayer today, I have all I need."

"Aren't you scared, being here in the dark?"

"Not at all, child," he replied. "The dark is perfect for crater-gazing. Why, just look at the moon tonight! Such luminous beauty!"

Rose saw how bright the moon & stars were against the night sky. I guess the dark can be helpful *and* beautiful, she thought.

They thanked Mr Brown & called at a few more houses, before heading back to the centre of the village. On their way they passed a pond. It was completely still & pitch black, save for tiny glimmers of light that were moving in a wave across the surface. It was a sparkle of fireflies, hundreds of them, moving in perfect unison, each one illuminating the tiny space around them, creating a beautiful glow.

"Just think," whispered the little ghost. "If it was daytime right now, we wouldn't have been able to see this!"

"That's true," Rose Witchling replied. Without the darkness, it would have gone completely unnoticed. I guess the dark can be helpful *and* beautiful *and* surprising, she thought.

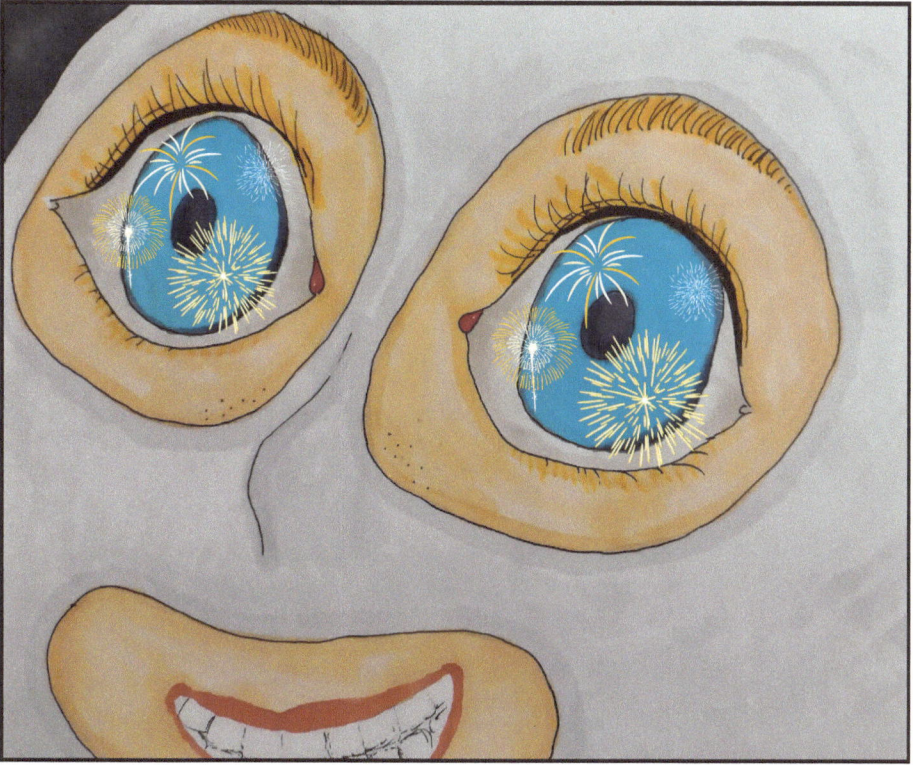

When they entered the village, most of the lanterns had been doused & there was a big crowd looking out towards the fields. Suddenly the night sky lit up in a luminous rainbow of fantastic colours. They were fireworks! Completely silent & as bright as the stars, they looked like pure magic against the night sky.

"I guess we wouldn't have seen these either if the sun was out," smiled the little ghost.

Rose Witchling nodded in agreement. I guess the dark can be helpful, *and* beautiful, *and* surprising, *and* useful, she thought.

Just then Rose Witchling spotted her family. "Where have you been, my little love?" asked Mama. "I've been Trick-or-Treating, and learning about the dark," Rose replied. "It's still a *bit* scary, but only a bit. It's also lots of other things! Like helpful, and beautiful, and useful. I guess it's a sort of necessary little-bit-scary-but-not-that-scary thing. You know?"

"I know," Mama returned with a smile. "I'm proud of you, my brave little Witchling, for facing your fear. Would you like to eat now?"

As Lily & Rose Witchling talked about all the different yummy soul cakes they had been given that evening, Mama prepared the Samhain Supper. Delicious roasted root vegetables & warm freshly-made bread, along with some sweet treats & homemade apple juice. The little ghost was so excited she could barely sit still in her seat. Mama lit some candles in the centre of the table & put her hands out towards the Witchlings:

"Blessed Be our loved ones & Blessed Be our friends,
A New Year is upon us & the Wheel has turned again,
We invite beloved ancestors to join us for this meal,
Generations long since past, the Goddess please reveal."

After the first wave of hunger had been sated, they began chatting about all the costumes they had seen in the village & all the different flavoured soul cakes they had been given. Rose told her Big Sister about the dark, & how it wasn't so scary after all.
"I'm so proud of you," said Lily Witchling. "Facing the things you're afraid of is very bold."
"And I'm proud of you both," said Mama. "For giving out so many prayers."
"And I'm proud to be a Pagan," said Rose. "It's so cool to have so many fun festivals to celebrate! Blessed Samhain, everyone!"

The
END!

SAMHAIN SOUL CAKE RECIPE

Ingredients:

- 175g (6oz) butter
- 175g (6oz) caster sugar
- 4 medium eggs
- 3 lemons

- 125g (4oz) self-raising flour
- 50g (2oz) ground almonds
- 75g (3oz) icing sugar
- 1 punnet of blueberries

Step 1: Preheat the oven to 180°c & line your loaf tin/oven dish with baking parchment.

Step 2: In a large bowl, beat together the butter & caster sugar with a hand-held electric whisk until pale & fluffy (this should take 3-5 minutes). Gradually beat in the eggs, followed by the finely grated zest of 2 lemons & the juice of 1 lemon.

Step 3: Fold the flour & ground almonds into the buttery mixture. Roll the blueberries in a spoonful of flour (this will prevent them all from sinking to the bottom of the cake during cooking) and add them in. Give it another mix.

Step 4: Spoon the batter into your prepared tin or oven dish and bake for 45 minutes or until a skewer can be inserted into the centre & comes out clean.

Step 5: Leave to cool in the tin for ten minutes & then turn onto a wire rack to cool down until *just* warm.

Step 6: Meanwhile put the icing sugar into a small bowl & stir in the juice of 2 lemons & the zest of the last lemon. Stir until smooth. Drizzle the icing onto the cake. Done!

TO STORE: Store in an airtight container for up to 4 days.

How to serve

This cake can be cut into anywhere between 12 & 21 pieces, depending on how thick you slice it!
Option 1 is to take a slice of Soul Cake & say a small prayer either to yourself or out loud for someone you love. Perhaps they need the Great Mother to bless their mental or physical health, their financial situation, or help get them through a tough time. Send them your love & energy as you eat.
Option 2 is to serve the Soul Cakes to trick-or-treaters when they call upon you for All Hallows Eve!

🦇Nutritionally, blueberries are full of fiber, vitamins C & K, & packed with antioxidants. Magically, they bless you with confidence, dream enhancement & aura cleansing.
🦇Lemons are full of vitamin C, potassium, calcium, & are excellent for the immune system. Magically, they provide purification, protection, and love, as well as clarity.
Blessed Be, dear reader! ✨

Did you enjoy this story?

LOOK OUT FOR MORE ADVENTURES IN THE TWO LITTLE WITCHLINGS SERIES!

- Yule
- Imbolc
- Ostara
- Beltane
- Litha
- Lammas
- Mabon

www.ingramcontent.com/pod-product-compliance
Lightning Source LLC
Chambersburg PA
CBHW040146070426

42448CB00032B/52